MW00637442

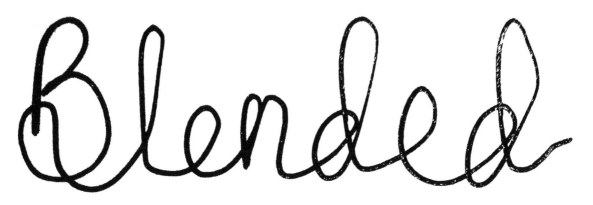

Blended

PERSPECTIVES ON BELONGING.

A PARTICIPATORY NOTEBOOK.

VELDA THOMAS

WITH ORIGINAL BLOCK PRINTS
BY THE AUTHOR

DEDICATION

This book is dedicated to the protectors and warriors who
    work with sacred truth.

May we live to feel one another's truths.
May we live to hear change coming.
May we live to smell the scent of freedom.
May we live to believe we are love.
May we live long enough to become ancestors singing in the
    wind.

With love,
Velda

TABLE OF CONTENTS

INTRODUCTION

A few years ago I began a journey with a voice that was new to me. The voice flowed forth with ease in the form of words on a page. Sparked by a thought, a sense impression or a story that kept drawing me back into its belly.

I wrote a series of essays and journal entries. Mostly stimulated by personal experiences that asked to be expressed — authentic, honest and raw. The deeper I went, the more complex and intersectional my thoughts became. Words distilled my process. Words helped me become more aligned with myself. Energy around words on the page sometimes surprises me, and I wonder if they are mine or my spirit muse speaking.

I call this body of work *Blended*.

Holding this book in my hands I recall my ancestors. Their names written in indigo ink within the records of the Catholic Church in the Caribbean. I see my great grandmother throwing bones on a dirt floor inviting me to join her group of Oracle readers in the spirit realm. Interacting with this text is a piece of history, her story and now our story, blended with the human story.

Offered as a place for readers to safely explore inner reflexes on topics of race, identity, belonging. The relationship is between my expression and your reading, digesting and journaling as needed, over days, months, years or a lifetime. Intended to create an intimacy between you and the text. Your creativity on the blank pages will be a personal evolution of this text. Pace yourself, take your time with the layers that surface.

I welcome you to explore the terrain in and around *Blended.*

USE OF THIS TEXT

These are suggestions for personal truth telling throughout this text:

Read the written pieces in order or not. Be free with your form.

Trust your intuition's inner response.

Try to replace judgement with interest.

Listen to your body's responses. Where in your body do you feel comfortable or uncomfortable? Ask your body why?

Express honestly, let your gut and heart connect with your mind.

Do not police or censor yourself. There is no right or wrong way to express.

It takes effort to dismantle and interrupt oppression starting within oneself.

Be in observation of outdated beliefs and habits.

When the inner critic begins to speak, push back, assert a boundary and continue to express.

Blank pages are for your reflection in creative form — to write, draw and create.

At the bottom of some of the blank pages I have offered reflection questions.

The text is also peppered with questions. Use them if they resonate with you. If not create your own open-ended questions.

To some individuals the text will be triggering. Be prepared to excavate your bias, privilege and judgements.

Reach out, connect and process feelings with trusted friends.

Find support groups. Work with a professional therapist.

Be gentle and kind to yourself during the learning process.

WHO AM I?

Who are you?
I am love's radical response to hate
Who are you?
I am the only one of me.
Who are you?
I am the first incarnation of myself.
Who are you?
I am the only one who can choose me.
Who are you?
I am the first love of my life.
Who are you?
I am the one link to break the chain.
Who are you?
I am the first, one and only that is enough.
Who are you?
I am the only deconstructor of my self-hatred.
Who are you?
I am cellular and the universe is me.
Who are you?
I am a creator, high on brave futurism.
Who are you?
I am a body that knows you.
Who are you?

LOSS

Loss opens the door and invites me near.
I whisper,
"If only I knew you were to disappear.
Be gone
From here.
Would I have acted differently?
Spent more time
Loved better
Been softer
Said more that needed to be said
Held you longer in my arms?
Maybe yes? Maybe no?
Now you have merged, become the essence of perfection in
    everything.
The warmth of the sun.
Wind gently swaying in tall grass.
A felt sense residing in that still between space."
Loss puts a palm on my back quietly assuring me.
"How well you loved.
You gave and received so openly. Holding nothing back.
I see that your tender heart functions perfectly and your
    flooding tears are now my worthy gems."
Hope intervenes singing with tenderness.
"Your grief is needed, welcome here.
Being left behind is a purposeful trial for the survivor.
A trail for the courageous barefoot warrior to tread."

Life is being carefully reinvented in your wake.
Without knowing how to proceed
I tend the seeds of your unconditional love and unwavering
    acceptance.
Paying the lessons forward.
Knowing now how perfect imperfection can be.
Practicing being that endless open kind of love.
May these seedlings rise strong.
Bridging worlds to one day become good ancestors reaching to
    us from the other side.
I whisper, louder this time from my heart into the ethers
Hoping you can hear my words.
"I always choose you again in the spirit realm dear one.
I'm lonely, longing to be with you for one more precious
    moment.
Please, message me?"
Meeting and separating are the flat sides of a spinning coin
    that in motion appear to be a sphere.
All that matters is love.
Love again, loving again and again.
May we meet again with our beloveds on the other side of this
    earthly shore.

Reflection

What have you lost?

What perfect imperfection can you learn to love?

BLENDED

Mixed, bi-racial, half caste, mulatto. If name calling happens
these are derogatory terms for what I am.

Within certain black thoughts I am rejected as a dilution of the
pure race. Within other ideologies — exotic, stronger for
mixing up the gene pool. Or a familial source of mystery
and shame.

Could this be a new genetic paradigm?

That we celebrate this mixed up hot mess of confusion that is
within us all.

Our one mongrel human race.

Cultural, racial, economic, complex beyond the stratosphere.

I am a half caste bastard born in 1965. Two years before
interracial marriage between black and white peoples
became legal in the US.

My relatives all look something like me. Shades of beautiful
brown skin.

Some you would never know have a black grandmother because
their blonde curls and blue eyes are so prominent.

Who do I choose to identify with?

Black, white, other?

I am not light enough to pass for white. Nor dark enough to be
purely black.

Surfing between worlds.

Which box shall I check today?

My naive self wants to deny the preference humans have for
bloodlines and breeding.

Dogs for example, seem to care about a dog being a dog.
Recognizing and embracing the inherent nature of their
species.
Is my wish to connect human to human too utopian?
Simple. Unrealistic.
My inner inquiry leads me to ask. What is MY current
prejudice or preference?
Can I dismantle racist tendencies living within and towards
myself? Acknowledge my bias.
Subtle self-hatred stemming from years of racial oppression
and fear wage war on the surface of my skin because of
what it means to be alive, of mixed blood and conscious.
DNA tests prove I am a pie graph of cultures within one body.
Most of us are. Right?
Truth be told, bias begins with sight. Seeing difference rather
than similarity. Blackness is demonized.
Media promotes desires for beauty and affluence that look a
certain way.
Is identity liberating or confining?
I can feel proud, power surging through for my blackness.
Other moments are full of pain, shame and grief where
otherness and belonging vie for space.
Will it ever be possible to move beyond these inner boundaries
so that embracing one another's otherness becomes the
norm?
When will that living myth become my truth?
There is no way for me to change the skin I was born into.
I'm living with more questions than answers.

Reflection

What boxes do you check today?
Are your identities liberating or confining?

COME UNITY

As a bi-racial woman.
I'm distrusting of community.
My bodily DNA demonstrates and lives segregation.
Pulling me inside to outside.
Othered for my whole life.
Becoming rigorously self-reliant to survive through
    generations of pain.
I refuse to rely on anyone.
Pridefully saying, "I'm a survivor."
Something precious has been lost.

Nesting within my nuclear family.
There is sadness, isolation and invisibility in a life
    without tribe.
What is the inner community?
Come unity.
I continue to separate from myself.
Hiding. Shrinking. Protecting.
Thinking that getting free meant being alone.
This body tells me that freedom is connecting to the
    holding of many who have no limits, expectations or
    judgments on my being.
I wait for my tribe to return for me.
Where are they?

Reflection

What have you survived?

Where do you seek community?

BODY TO BODY

In the darkness of night I am awake. Heat, sweat pouring, heart racing, thoughts swirling.

Am I safe?

My brown body orator speaks to herself.

"I am your mother. I am your father. I am body so beautiful containing precise but uncontrollable primal chaos in order to be born of self repeatedly. Turning inside out for imaginative perspectives.

My wise knowing, holding and protecting of you is ever transforming. Flesh, bone and elements constantly shifting to fit you better. Steady unwinding of my outer and inner resistance continues to inform you.

The invitation to reside within my fertile garden womb of energy through this gestation still stands.

Always turn towards me, your body, when seeking. My universe has all the answers you will ever need.

I am your first home.

This skin is flexible and can hold all of you.

Your need to escape and elude me is fear of the knowledge bodily truth carries within your DNA.

I urge you to live that truth.

Ancestors speak by manifesting active desires through you.

Embrace your thickened knuckles and scarred joints — for you are here to inhabit me fully.

Resistance is futile. The time of constructing defenses is over for you and I.

Embed unity and solidarity into the functions of your organs.
The mind is safely strong in its own illusion.
This deep body holds the vast freedom you so desire.
Follow your soul inward to become one with me.
The origin of all purpose is LOVE.
I want you to believe that you can soften, be vulnerable and let
    many years of dammed up tears flow.
Because you are not a mistake.
You can scream to the high heavens to shake the numbness
    awake.
Because you are not wrong.
You can moan to the pit of your belly unearthing buried
    memories, secrets stored no one knew you would ever
    reveal.
Because the body cannot lie.
Like the snake shedding its skin, the layers fall away year after
    year as you grow more into your divinity.
Please believe me.
I'm listening to you.
I am not your true skin.
I am your body.

Reflection

How does the body inform action?

What conditions are necessary to hear the body speak?

JOY

A joy fountain of diamonds bubbling, spiraling up through
   my body.

Was I on drugs? A giddy woman child.

I shut it down immediately.

NO. Not that much joy.

NO. Not for me.

My wounded, abused ass only gets to suffer.

Then my muse chimed in.

"Hey girl.

Uh uh, you don't get to shut that down.

Don't shut down your shine.

Revel in that sweet perfume."

Now. Listen up. People.

When you see me feeling power.

Emanating love's wonder.

Sprinkling joy dust on trails.

Raise me up.

Be curious about the mischief in my eyes.

Because my joy, is your joy, is our joy.

Reflection

Where do you find joy?
Where do you give joy?

WHAT'S MINE

My love
My joy
My Queendom
My pleasure
Are you interested?

My needs
My rules
My time frame
My power
Are you available?

My gifts
My blackness
My spirit
My legacy
Are you willing to amplify me?
Because all I hear is your voice.

I wrote this poem after the murder of yet another black man at the hands of law enforcement officers.

In the time and place that will occupy space in tomorrow's history books — where the world watched marches burst forth from quarantine and riots tumble through major US cities.

Eventually touching the world.

White people wearing the fresh pain of witnessing murder frantically bought books, watched movies, scoured the internet for sources to heal the raw wound in themselves called systemic racism.

While for many black bodies the murder of black men is nothing new. Grief became numbness which turned into anger and rage.

Oppression has been created over lifetimes and centuries. It is not likely to be fixed in a minute by a new found popular sense of urgency to end racism across the globe.

The healer in me knows that mass acknowledgement and participation in healing on an individual level must be the first step to create movement sending ripples of change into the collective consciousnesses.

This brand of healing requires personal engagement in dismantling systems of white supremacy and colonialism within every human body.

Digging deeper still.

Engaging in the righteous battle with the inner demons of greed, hatred and dominance. Winning means humanity might emerge to create love, respect, equality and justice for all beings.

I have become tired of seeing examples of beautiful black ideas, black livelihood, black joy being overshadowed in the media by continual images of hate, pain and violence towards black bodies.

I took an early evening bike ride in an attempt to shift this pent up energy coursing through my body.

I chanted the words over and over to the trees as I pushed the pedals home.

Asking the universe why the simple pure acts of black self-love, black joy, black pleasure and black beauty are not being amplified.

These are the unrecognized qualities in black bodies that are the continuous living acts of rebellion towards oppression leading to inner freedom.

It is important to keep laughing, singing, dancing, connecting, creating and loving what pleases the black human body.

For that is loving living.

To expand upon my poem, I invite you in the spirit of freedom to live into the creative space of questions.

No need to rush to an answer.

There is no right or wrong.

It's all about what is your living truth.
How are you an evolving human?
Sit still.
Wait. Be patient.
Answers will emerge.

My love
My joy
My queendom
My pleasure
Are you interested?

When black people show power do we feel threatened?
Envious?
A sense of lack?
Is the world interested in knowing and supporting black joy?
Does self-interest dominate / undermine the act of curiosity
    and authentic human connection?

My needs
My rules
My time frame
My power
Are you available?

Do we believe black people deserve support?
Are there conditions to your availability for support?
Judgements. Areas of life black successes can or can't be?
What giving archetype are we comfortable with?

Saving, helping, enabling, co-dependent, sharing, hand
  holding? Or gifting?

My gifts
My blackness
My spirit
My legacy
Are you willing to amplify me?
Because all I hear is your voice.

Invisibility is one of racism's festering wounds, blotting out /
  silencing people of color whose gifts are in clear view.

Power is palpable and joy is free.
However pain and suffering have an intriguing allure to most
  humans.
What qualities are amplified?
Is it the norm to amplify black suffering and pain?
How does our culture celebrate black health, black love,
  success, family and joy?

Now is the time to change the pain narrative. To create a new
  narrative where all peoples can fit at the table, look one
  another in the eye, and say YES we will all do this and we
  can all do better by telling the truth and working through
  our part in the cycles of trauma and pain. Naming and
  claiming what's mine is one way I'm loving myself fiercely
  on this journey towards liberation.

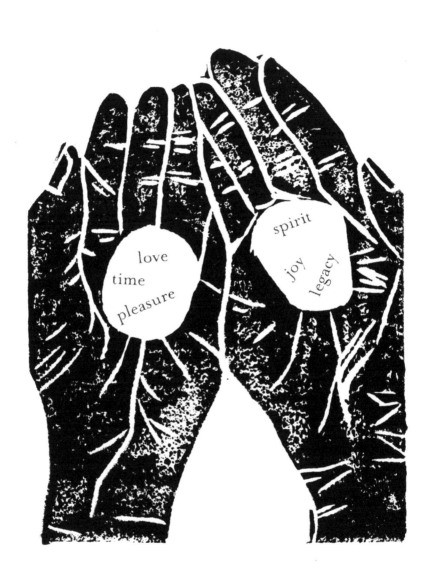

Reflection

What has been invisible to you?

What are you willing to amplify?

CULTURAL MANIFESTO

Ancestors are feverish cooking up cultural uprisings.
Exposing gold veins of generational trauma so healing may
    begin.
Remember, reclaim and reinvent what is lost.
Manifest for yourself first.
Inwardly directed clear spiritual eyes.
Take pride in origination imagination.
Forge a life full of new costumes gathered in personal dream
    time.
Speaking mother's tongues.

Sink connective roots deep into the soil.
There is a place on earth for you that is called home.
Amplify pride, pleasure and joy.
Diasporas' intersecting healing paths imbibe much needed
    medicine.
Evaporating energy into the ethers to affect us all.
No more separate, divide and conquer.
In unity we thrive.

Reflection

What can you reclaim that has been lost?

Describe the place you feel most at home?

A BROWN BROWNIE

There was a five-year-old self that is still lurking somewhere
within. She was willful, cheeky, confident and tastefully
spicy.
That Velda was a new brand of naughty to her proper West
Indian family.
Secretly locking herself in the bathroom for an hour when
asked to call her mother's new beau's parents Grandma and
Grandpa.
She dug her heels in for truth telling.
These people had just arrived. Who were they?
He was not her Grandpa and she was not "Nanny."

Feeling a creative urge, child Velda rubbed Vaseline over a
bedroom wall in the new grandparents' home.
She was supposedly napping.
Five-year-old Velda was funny, nosey, mischievous with a dash
of wild.
Looking back through my child lens. I time travel to recall
what happened during that winter.

Cold damp frosty evenings were the norm in England. Getting
dressed up in a crimplene brown dress with white knee
highs, topped off with a brown felt beret.
Bundling up to dwell within a musty dark church hall. To
attend my first Brownie meeting.
(Brownies are the younger part of the Girl Guides
organization)

Really, I was joining a gang.
I felt special as if I had been chosen to be a Brownie.
Friends. Activities, games, outings and contests. Badges upon
  badges to stitch on my small brown dress.
If I was a good girl. Helped my Mum at home. Performed
  tasks with dog-like obedience.
I was rewarded with a pin or an embroidered badge.
I was hooked by the system.

Then there was the play.
I received a beautiful book of fairy tales for Xmas so I knew
  this one all too well.
Snow White.
The story goes.
A wicked jealous queen orders the murder of her innocent
  stepdaughter. Snow White escapes and hides in the woods
  with seven little people. She disguises herself as a hag. The
  queen is enraged to find out Snow White is alive.
She gifts a poisoned apple to Snow White who falls into a
  coma of sleep. The spell can only be broken by the kiss of a
  prince.

Months of rehearsals, costume and set design. Apprehension
  building. Finally the day came when all the Brownies were
  assigned parts.
Excitement building in every pore of my body.
In my mind I was clearly going to be Snow White.
I knew all the lines.
Could sing the song.

My family always called me a star princess. Lying came
  naturally so acting was meant for me.

Right?
WRONG.
The words *gardener* and *donkey* connected to Velda hit me in the
    pit of my stomach.
I was expected to play those roles.
Nothing in me understood how this could happen.
This was a soul crushing blow.
My mood became salty and poured out without apology.
I was grumpy, rude and refused to participate in the parts
    chosen for me. Nothing could convince me that I was not
    Snow White worthy. The girl chosen to play Snow White
    received a good measure of my side-eye spice.
"Why not? Why couldn't I be Snow White?"

No one answered my question.
The poison of verbal abuse ensued when the white woman
    leader of the Brownie troupe told me that I was obstinate
    and ungrateful for not being compliant.
I determined that she would never be the boss of me.
I convinced myself not to care. Reinforcing the impact of her
    thoughtless action. The intent was to discipline without
    harm.
Innocence was lost and distrust took its place.

My mother was embarrassed and disappointed after the play. I
    refused to go back and endure more abuse.
Or maybe the Brownies did not want me.
I don't remember talking to my mother about that experience.
In our family Snow White died and was swept under the rug
    and forgotten.
Except.
A body blueprint established itself and did not forget.
Full of violent messaging. Toxicity's booming voice went like
    this.

"You are not white.
You are deemed not worthy.
You are seen as not good enough.
Your contribution has no value.
You are not wanted here.
You are other. Not like us."
The reality of western beauty standards still visible today
    dropped into my body imprinting.
"Darker is lesser, undesirable and ugly."

Unraveling this experience now I see the obvious.
It's 1970.
How could a brown girl Brownie, me, ever play the part of
    Snow White?
The beautiful thing is that back then at five years old I didn't
    know what black, brown or white skin meant.
I saw friends, animals, plants. Family wrapped me in
    goodness. Loved me for being a first grandchild.
I was shocked, surprised, astonished to learn that the color of
    my skin was not desirable everywhere.
The structures in place professed that Snow White was the
    perfect beauty. She was not brown.
If I could've jumped into a white skinsuit. Child Velda would
    have sold herself to play the part of Snow White.

The perfect part for Velda had not yet been scripted and no
    auditions were being held.
What I learned was a brand of subtle self-loathing for my own
    skinsuit.
One thing I know is that I can never get out of this skin.
I will be in this skin until I die.
At that time I toughened this skin to protect myself from more
    pain.

Now looking at photos of my child self before and after
    this event I believe I perceive something subtle was lost,
    changed, gone forever.
The sassy, confident child dissolved. Disappeared. Erased.
The Velda after was contracted, quiet, trying to fit in. She
    worried about what people thought of her.
Compounding life circumstances made her feel as if her very
    existence was wrong.

A mistake.

In my current imagination I hold that smaller version of
    Velda's spirit in close kindness and whisper tender words
    in her ear. I introduce her to the confident full essence of
    Velda.
They live side by side as comrades expanding authentically,
    filling the universe. Lifting clouded veils so the cathartic
    process of truth telling emerges to move energies.
I now claim and cast my own role in the magical fairytale of a
    life where this story, too, belongs.

Reflection

What toxic messages did you receive in your childhood?
What have you learned about beauty?

BLACK PIONEERS

Black Pioneers practice love.

Black Pioneers live firsts.

Black Pioneers change narratives.

Black Pioneers envision beyond now.

Black Pioneers demonstrate truth telling.

Black Pioneers challenge boundaries.

Black Pioneers accentuate courage.

Black Pioneers practice humility.

Black Pioneers are originals.

Black Pioneers lift each other up.

Black Pioneers polish their shine.

Black Pioneers establish new territories.

Black Pioneers are futuristic for all humanity.

I don't know

Reflection

Who are your Pioneers?
What have you pioneered?

RAINY TEARS

Experiences become memories swirl underwater and then rise
   to float on the surface for a while.
Let's go back a spell.
"Today, I kept my promise. I returned to a music stall in the
   Medina to buy instruments.
The tiny shop was chocked full of fascinating foreign objects.
   Prepared to haggle for the best price which is all part and
   parcel of the social task when shopping in Marrakech.
Buying was extra appealing today because of the downpour
   from the heavens.
At the music stall Zachariah makes me tea, maybe a tactic
   seducing me to buy more?
But let's go with it anyway.
We sit together in his tiny shop. He plays some of the
   instruments and I listen with eyes closed and ears open,
   feeling unfamiliar but familiar rhythms in my hands
   and feet.
Joy moves my feet and I offer a small dance to the music in the
   middle of the tiny shop.
Hands on his heart. Zach bows his head to me in thanks. Then
   business begins or so I think.
Zach asks me. "Have you heard about the origin of this
   instrument?" A metal pair of hand percussion instruments.
Gambri played in the traditional Gnaoua music.
I say "Please tell me, I want to know."
Zach's story begins.

"Long ago there were people taken from their country of
     origin. Slaves.
They were captured and wore shackles. Searching for answers
     to their misfortune.
Asking themselves.
Why is this happening to me? Why am I taken from my family
     that I love? Why am I black?
Why is this god's will for me? Why do I have to suffer so?
How will I bear all this pain? Maybe I will die here.
The slaves bound in those chains made rhythms by hitting the
     metal shackles that bound their feet and hands together.
They sang their songs to the heavens. This clanging rhythm
     intended to transcend their suffering, ease their pain and
     bring them into trance, reaching for another dimension
     beyond the physical realm.
The slaves left their bodies behind. The music they created
     kept them alive.
Souls connected and spirits were fed by the food of music.
The slaves could endure another day."

The instrument was a reminder to me of the pain, survival
     and resilience of all captured slaves.
There were those with warrior spirits that chose death.
     Jumped overboard never to be oppressed and abused. I am
     a descendant of the ones that suffered, gained strength and
     survived.

After Zach's story I felt the African American slaves in my body.
I could hear voices field hollering on sugar and cotton
     plantations. I could feel the origin of the Blues.
I shared these facts with Zach. I surprised myself as tears
     rolled down my cheeks. I had opened my heart to a dark
     place that was previously hardened to me.

I felt deep ancestral suffering coursing in my veins. Zach
 rubbed his face unsure of this intimate sharing with a total
 stranger. Our eyes meet and he, too, is crying. He tells me a
 fraction of his orphaned life story. Together our tears flow
 more and more. The burdens alive within are released for a
 spell of time.
He is a salesman. We are no longer strangers to one another.
 We laugh and cry and drink mint tea.
I buy my instruments, we hold hands and say our tender
 goodbye blessings.

I may never be here or see him again.
I leave with my heart open and mind refreshed.
Back to the streets of Medina.
Moroccan rain washes away the salty dry tear stains still on
 my face.
Some memories are burdens and some like this are a blessing.

Reflection

When and how do ancestors communicate through you?
Which healing tears have you shed?

A BRIEF FRIENDSHIP

The Millers were more curious about my husband and me than
 we were about them. We met Mary and Doug Miller on a
 road trip to Montana in 1996.
Our journey took us further into the wild open country of
 western America.
Leaving urban Seattle behind in the rain.

The Millers' curiosity got the better of them.
VW camper rig? Suggested hippies.
English accent? Sounded other: foreigners.
Seattle people? Warned of city behaviors.
We learned that Mary's dream was to one day see the Pacific
 Ocean. Doug was born on the land he lived on.
A salt of the earth farmer his whole life.

I spent my days in the Montana countryside walking, picking
 wild flowers and poking around out-buildings across from
 their home, enjoying vast views, big skies and long grass at
 my feet. The America of western movies long imagined was
 real.
As a child in suburban England I had transported myself via
 TV to the plains on rainy Sunday afternoons.
Now I was there.

A wave. A smile. A word or two.
We became acquainted with one another.

Especially when I wanted to experience a ride on the Millers'
    chestnut horse.
Doug made sure the mare was safe by getting his old bones in
    the saddle for a jog before he let me ride her.
They invited us over to their home across the dirt road for
    coffee. We chatted about our city life and learned that their
    family homesteaded the land they lived on. Real, living
    pioneers. Our ancestors had land, hard work and struggle
    in common.

The following week Mary insisted on making us pie.
We agreed on cherry and went to visit again.
I understood the loneliness of remote living and what it's like
    to long for female company.
I happily obliged her with visits during our six week stay.
She told me the stories of her life. Shared scrapbooks of their
    100 year history on the land.
Long ago they lived in a one room shack during the harsh
    Montana winter. Eating pigeons and squirrels to survive,
    they were so poor.

I followed Mary to help out in the kitchen while the men
    talked.
Conversation flowed with ease.
Our laughter dotted through friendly chatter.
Mary said, "Can I tell you something?"
I replied, "Absolutely."
She quietly shared. "You are the first black woman I've ever
    spoken to in all my years."
I didn't know what to say.
Mary continued. "I see black women in the supermarket with
    their beautiful children. I want to say hello, but never have."

The first thing that struck me was her courage and
honesty. Under that I sensed in her a tinge of hidden
embarrassment, even shame for being so open with her
buried thoughts that could not be taken back.
I replied, "I'm glad you told me that." I was honored and at the
same time strangely wary to be her confidante.
My body calibrated taking in what she had revealed.
In my slow-to-process rhythm, many thoughts raced through
my blood over the following days.
I didn't say much. Mary was my elder. I had been taught not to
question those fortunate enough to reach that rank.
My safety felt unclear.
On an unconscious level was my survival in question?

Black women protect in subtle ways. Stepping in front. Taking
a blow. Or opting for silence.
I didn't want to hurt or call attention to a gesture that seemed
innocent enough to me. To another black woman her
sharing could have been highlighted as stupidity.
The same way commenting on skin tone, beauty and racial
stereotypes might be a tipping point for negative social
interactions.

For me, Mary was also a first.
The first openly racist white woman I had met.
Or was she racist?
Or the first to show me that segregation still lives?
Or the first to bridge the space between us?
The first white woman of her generation to admit that her
desire to connect was greater than the desire for separation.

During our time together, I shared details of my family's
pioneering endurance.
So many firsts.

First to leave the small Caribbean islands.
First to settle in a small English town.
First black kids in schools.
First interracial marriages.
First to never get to see their parents again.
First to die in a foreign land.
We continued eating pie, chatting and drinking cowboy coffee.
Something profound had transpired in those moments.
I'd have to name it as curiosity, innocence and vulnerability
    leading me to grace, tolerance, acceptance.
Even love. I will never know if Mary felt the same.
Those words of truth we had exchanged in the kitchen,
    woman to woman, sealed our brief friendship.

Doug showed me his dowsing skills with pride, assuring me
    that I too must have the gift of feeling the water.
The Millers embraced me with tenderness as I gifted them
    time and company.
Inviting me to accompany them to place flowers on their
    family gravesites on Memorial Day.
We ate ice cream together afterwards in the local diner. I could
    feel their protection towards me as we drove through town.
Maybe Mary shed a tear I didn't see when we said goodbye.
Am I too romantic?

Part of the truth is that these very people in their limited
    experience were capable of harming black bodies.
Without hateful intent. More so out of fear for the OTHER.

Thinking back now, I recall my time in Montana with a
    mixture of fondness and hesitation.
Fondness for the land. The feeling of freedom. The energy
    of pioneers. Hesitation for the proximity to a kind of

whiteness I had never experienced.

Youth and my comfort with the kind of British whiteness I
grew up with made me oblivious to the dangers of being
black in a small, unfamiliar white American community.

Aware that I fought the urge to shrink, be overly humble or
slipping into joking and entertaining to create comfort.

Performing labors invisible to others but impactful for myself.

I worked to be palatable, friendly, bringing all parts of me
to the present.

Maybe our black farmer friend we were visiting broke the ice.
Maybe he broke the Millers' view of stereotypes.

Maybe they had a new understanding that black people are
individuals with varied life experiences.

Not simply the stories made visible by the media.

I hold this story tight. Sharing now because I believe that
finding personal courage to create pathways for connection
and interaction with "others" are the keys to experiencing
that humans are more similar than different.

I believe we had a lot in common with the Millers.

We all enjoyed cherry pie.

Mary and Doug Miller are now long gone from this earth.

I thank them for their curiosity and for sharing the bright sun
and blue spring skies of Montana.

May they rest in peace.

Reflection

How is a cultural bridge created between people?
When can compassion win?

BELOVED BLACK MEN

I'm feeling the mighty spirit protector rising in my chest for
   men of color.
It's a fierce signal registered within DNA, ovaries of great
   greats whose wombs I lay within.
Ancestral traumas brewing for centuries triggered here and
   now.
Sometimes confusion reigns and trauma is too deep to turn
   toward, let alone feel.
"I am numb."

There are subtle dangers for brown-black male bodies in a
   laid-back liberal small town.
Historically a white woman has privileged super powers.
She can say the "word" and folks will gather, hunt and do
   bodily harm in a righteous frenzy to brown-black-skinned
   truth.
No questions asked.
"I am sickened."

Let's get real. Only melanin stereotypes are welcome. The
   needy, exotic, druggy, pimp, mute, orderly, athlete, comic,
   musician and compliant fool might be accepted into the
   "white crew" and typecast in a role to play.
"I am disgusted."

"Black" men.
Punished for fear that they are too ....?
Our collective cultural sickness wrapped around "race" is a
    chronic hot mess.
Betrayal is real and brown-black bodies are being socially and
    emotionally lynched.
The desire to awaken in the collective liberal mind is
    dormant, unconscious.
In denial.
"I am enraged."

Brown-black men understand in their bones it is precarious
    to be alive. Any act can be contorted and used against.
History tells of a humanity tying you up, locking you in or
    shackling you down.
To open up, speak out, be oneself is unnecessary risk taking.
    Vulnerability surely gives rise to victimhood.
Never lay down the weapons. Defend oneself at all cost
    because it appears on some level we are always at war.
One escape route is to flee the situation, body and soul into
    isolated invisibility.
"I am hurting."

To be real, flawed, strong and authentic in self-loving brown-
    black skin.
Tell me. Is this a crime?

I remember holding my brown boy, during his first days of
    life. Surprised at the heavy weight pressing on my soul,
    I sobbed, hormones rushing. Heart bursting for all the
    possible misunderstood actions of others coming for him
    on a path yet unveiled.
He is a perceived danger. Brown baby boy.

Is it my job to steer destiny or protect you?
Will hard knocks ultimately serve in his survival?
I'm ashamed of my timing being off.
Gut responding after the facts and acts.
I'm his brown mother.
Still learning my own overridden complexities.
I want to tattoo a knowing onto his soul.
A knowing of his divine essence mixed with all the wrongness
    in the world.
You are a shining star.
Heads up!
Space for your true freedom is narrow here.
"I am real."

Our black brown boys can be dazed, bleeding at the side of
    the road. Cars drive by but nobody stops to find out if a
    12-year-old brown boy needs help.
He's invisible unless he's angry.
Asking with his kind, smiling bright eyes.
"Mama. Why can't they see?
It's just me."
But it's no longer just you.
You are becoming a man-child.
Learning you can't always be what you are.
Perfect, vulnerable and expressive.
Forging yourself for this black life.
"I am truth."

People please. Acknowledge and challenge the racist part of
    self.
Have the courage to voice truth and be conscious in action.
Stop the cycles brimming out of fearful self-loathing.
For this will rot a human from the inside out.

Keep the dangerous unconscious shadow of fear at bay and in
   check at all times.
Lest fear rule the majority and we all fall prey to the death
   chambers.
"I am courage."

Can forgiveness ever happen? Maybe in time when atrocities
   have been acknowledged, apologies expressed and honest
   amends made. Generations born and buried. Possibly
   gratitude will surface and the pain of experience be
   composted into the alchemy of future wisdoms.

I know that within my lineage of spirit infused brown-black
   people, beyond all strategy and complexity is a strength
   so vast, a heart source so unconditional it can choose to
   embrace all the chaotic human polarities at once or not.
"I am human."

The sheath that protects this current body I reside within
Is my golden brown skin.
I keep trying to experience my skin holding me.
It's exhausting.
"I am afraid."

Reflection

Who knows a black man's pain or truth?

Who unconditionally sees our black boys and men?

MAMMY

I.

Nancy Agnes Elfrieda Jeffrey was all black matriarch and my
    grandmother.
I called her *Nanny.*
All the adults around me called her *Mammy.*
Her own children called her *Mammy.*
Her husband called her *Mammy.*
In my youth I accepted this as my grandmother's other name.
There was even an endearing quality to the ear when people
    called out to her: *"Mammy!"*

I remember my grandmother's smile. A glow like the warmth
    of the sun turning honey to liquid sweetness. Or the shy
    sun peeking out from behind a cloud to let you know warm
    days are coming.

I remember Elfrieda's hymn and hum as she cleaned the
    house, did laundry and herded her grandchildren, hanging
    onto her apron strings day in, day out.
I remember laying my head on her pillow-like thighs.
Enveloped into her softness.
The smell of baking lingering on her apron as she hummed
    me to rest with enduring love.

I remember being locked between her strong knees for the

dreaded daily hair combing routine.

My tender head crying out to meet her response.

"Child, beauty is pain."

Nancy had super powers with fire. Heat of discipline from
her eyes that stopped me from continuing any childish
naughtiness. Truly, she possessed spider senses and eyes in
the back of her head.

With one look, I was burned into submission.

I remember Agnes's fondness for Jim Reeves' country music.
Wrestling. Rum. Chicken. Bright colored flowers, and her
family. Her family. Her family.

Mrs. Thomas had faith. Hours of devotion in church
accumulated into years.

Dressed to the nines, I helped choose which Sunday fancy hat
she'd wear from her wardrobe of many.

Watching her hit the ground in prayer. Possessed by the
Holy Spirit. Hearing her speak in tongues was a natural
occurrence for me.

I remember the day she told me she had nurtured white
people's children for money.

Those people called her *Mammy.*

Willingly she gave them her unconditional love and comfort.

The trauma of her life became visible in her brokenness.

Sitting quietly in an armchair for hours rocking back and
forth hugging herself, she began to disappear before
my eyes.

Mental illness brought rage, mood swings and hurtful verbal
outbursts towards those who loved her most.

Eventually hospitalized and medicated to become a shell of her
former self.

Dementia set in.

All the joy used up, gone.
Poof.
Life numbed for her final years.

The woman I describe here was so much more than a
    construct caricature called *Mammy*.
Nancy Agnes Elfrieda Jeffrey was mine. A part of the conduit
    for my being here. I lay in her womb, too.
We still continually reach for each other. She from the other
    side, me towards her from this physical reality where she
    willingly now embodies the role of my spiritual matriarchal
    ancestor.
Nancy Agnes Elfrieda Jeffrey.

Reflection

Develop an imagination of your super power.

What from the ancestors informs you now?

II.

The other at your service *Mammy* is a homely, happy slave.
　　Ebony skinned, fat woman with large breasts.
Wearing a maids uniform. A gingham kerchief to cover her
　　unkempt head of hair.
White Imagination says that she was more dedicated to her
　　white family than her own kin.
BULLSHIT
Mammy was deemed a house slave. White property only suitable
　　for long hours of domestic work.

The other do it all *Mammy.*
Maid, cook, fixer, caregiver, listener, cleaner, wet nurse.
Aunt Jemima, Beulah, Delilah.
White Imagination says that she joyfully labored long and hard
　　while singing her daily slave contentment song with a smile
　　on her face.
BULLSHIT
Mammy used her body to curate an invisible holding pen big
　　enough for everyone to dump their suffering in.

The other suck it up *Mammy.*
Renamed by the house. Then portrayed as simple and
　　illiterate. Speaking unrefined broken English. Full of
　　religious fervor and old time superstitions. Appearing
　　utterly content to do her white families bidding.

White imagination dictated that she maintained good humor as long as her "good fortune" remained to belong to systemic oppression.

BULLSHIT

Mammy is where Antebellum's black female slave was placed to exist in the illusion of safety.

The other sex slave *Mammy* would never be exotic, clever, beautiful, powerful and cultured. Her wild essence is forbidden except to pleasure another.

Rejecting the attention of the oppressor is a punishable crime.

White imagination says that white dominance had the right to enact desires in order to remain intact and secure by any means necessary.

BULLSHIT

The mistress of the house needed to use *Mammy's* magic for her desires, too.

Black women have exhibited enough bandwidth to face hatred and unconditionally demonstrate love.

Holding polarity perfectly in one palm.

Black women are exhausted.

Black women are accustomed to silent requests for unpaid invisible labor. Keeping the status quo so those around them experience ease and comfort.

Systems in place make it impossible to stop performing free labor that takes a toll on frayed emotions.

Piling more of a load upon an already trauma laden nervous system. Ancestral. Generational.

Physical, emotional and trau-more.

Is this what holding the title *Mammy* means?

BULLSHIT

Mammy is also a testament to the black human spirit. As a people we made it through abusive hatred while somehow managing to channel rage into creative brilliance without burning everything to the ground.

All while building for new spiritual pathways to thrive.

There is pride in *Mammy's* survival and evolution.

Reflection

What comes of hatred?

How does love transform evil?

III.

The *Mammy* I want to favor growing in me is a wild card.
Today I rename her Ellibet.
She is primal in ways that are complex, practical and
    earthbound.
Following instinctual somatic responses to key into intuition's
    messages.
Unbothered, unapologetic and unpredictable.
Minding her drama-less business.
Original within old forms.
Seeking no one's approval.
Ellibet is the boss of her world.
She is strong, deep, potent, too intense for some timid souls.
She rolls naked on the earth.
Laughing as she rises with leafy debris embedded in her locks.
Playfully inappropriate for reactions sake.
Story does not define Ellibet.
She is an energy shifter and shape changer.
Singing her wordless songs to the sun, stars and moon.
Giving herself permission to shriek and giggle in private
    pleasure.
Landing in the sweet spots of blessed silence to meet her
rightful size.
Ellibet can be called upon day, night and in the ethers.
Needing no audience for validation.

Lived wisdom of the heart, body and spirit are her valued
    forms of education.
She is a bridge balancing between seen and unseen worlds
    inhabiting her body as a loving sanctuary.

The pendulum swings in the other direction and I find
    myself here.
Sitting with the other *Mammy* in me.
The tension of resistance is ever present in my body as I locate
    the spot *Mammy* resides in today.
I fillet myself open exposing hypertonic muscle due to holding
    oppression in too tightly.
Is pain now centered on display for voyeurs?
Are these word spells branding or liberating me?
I can only know what I know until I know better.
I take a dose of courage and land on the razor's edge of my
    vulnerability.
My domesticated self is a slave.
Another part of me also holds the position of slave master
    and overseer.
This part of me has become driven by self imposed inbuilt
    expectations of physical and emotional labor.

 What would my *Mammy* slave name be?
There is no name.
She's a heavy blanket soothing anxiety and applying constant
    pressure to keep me tucked into dominant culture's
    acceptable boxes.
Lack of safety manifests as appearing energetically contracted.
Head hung low. Body caving in with hurt.
This *Mammy* does exactly what she is told. Asks for nothing and
    expects less in return.

Is overly humble. Apologetic.
Showing little emotion because she's scared to draw attention
    to herself.
She's been shamed and punished into submission.
Growing to be most comfortable with the uncomfortable.
It is impossible to see who *Mammy* in me really is.
The masks of truth, lies and perception weave their own web
    to sit within.
Black bold genius is invisible even to me.

Mammy in me wants to shout, whisper, moan, laugh, or cry.
But in reality this *Mammy* is muted. She cannot find a space to
    thrive.
I wonder. Where did this narrative come from?
Ahhhh. I laid comfortably in the wombs of those who lived as
    Mammy before me.
I am hard wired to suffer in silence, do more and bare pain in
    order to survive.
The slave master and overseer in me keep the forms of self
    oppression securely in place.

Somewhere there is a space in between where *Mammy* in me
    lives the dance with these two characters.
The dance of dissonance. Where disruption of oppression can
    take place.
Imagining graceful arms expanding into sovereignty.
    Footwork. Leading to a self governing clear state of being.
Gaze. Becoming self determined forging her desired path.
Stature. Her true worth and value are known presenting
    choice and ownership of self.
Building joy through self love. This medicine applied to the
    pain of oppression becomes the healing balm for *Mammy's*
    soul.

I recognize her.
I am more.
I am bigger.
I am vocalizing my own legacy.

Note. In my writing thus far "Mammy" was gendered as a woman, but now gender fluid so that all bodies may find an aspect of "Mammy" within.

Reflection

How is wild vs domesticated expressed in you?
Where is your balance point?

IV.

Mammy

BREATHE
Inhale. Exhale.

Stop a minute. Take off your apron. Let out a sigh and step
over the threshold into your one beautiful bodily home.
Your black skin.
Rest here, rub those tired feet. Smile with pride, gratitude and
joy. You have endured much for the many. Imagination
living in your blood has fed generations with dreams of
freedom.
All those compassionate gifts showered on others are for you,
too. Cradle your steady beating heart in those weathered
hands while things move and change.

Holding onto one another in a fluid cosmic gaze. We are one.
Magnifying a view of the spirit's future in microscopic detail
through the mind's eye.
Our eyes meet and souls meld.
In your black pupil, a universe of messages flow through
intended for all who recognize *Mammy* in their broken
souls.
Close your eyes.

BREATHE
Inhale. Exhale.

Ritual time begins.
Brokenness is witnessed by a willingness to rest.
Permission is granted to step into eternities and pain
    consciousness together.
Carefully blowing centuries of festering suffering away with
    the smoke of ancient scented herbs,
Cauterizing open wounds and applying the long needed
    sacred balms of compassion and self love
Before wrapping burdensome injuries with a spiders web of
    the finest courage.
Nurturing tea blends brew in a pot full of value, self worth,
    autonomy and belonging.
Tears begin to flow.
Joy for life is breaking through a well built dam for the first
    time.

Divinity speaks into *Mammy*.

"Please believe these words.
I love you. I love everything about you. I love all of you.
I'm so sorry this happened to you. You did nothing to deserve
    being treated as lesser than.
I gift you your own forgiveness for your participation.
Dip yourself in its cleansing water washing away any residual
    shame.
Praise to you for all profits paid forward. Assisting to ensure
    humanity's survival.
Thank you for existing."

BREATHE

Inhale. Exhale.

The mission ahead is to completely liberate, deconstruct and integrate *Mammy*.
Cutting through thick emotions with crystalline precision.
Healing too now belongs.
Wrapped in meditative word spells projecting us into other dimensions.
Finally there is space for sweet relief.
Delicately past *Mammy* is laid to rest in the strong loving arms of a mountain range.
Could healing be this simple?
Mammy can never be forgotten.
Mammy is accepted, seen, heard and released from all existing binding contracts.
Jump up. Shout out.
Celebrate.
Ayyyyah Karrumba!!!
They are free.
Fly free.
Be Free.

Reflection

What unseen contracts bind you?

How can choice and safety equate freedom?

IN SERVICE

A sunny day. I was walking my dog. My own thoughts
    frightened me. It went like this.
"If I am not giving to others, who am I and what is my
    purpose?"
My heart sank into the pit of my belly. I felt utterly lost for a
    few minutes.
I answered myself with, "Well. You'd be dead."
Panicked, I fled. Stuffing emotions into my body. Stored for
    another time that would take me closer to the truth buried
    within this thought. Knowing that I am a good survivor of
    the past's wounds.

On my grandfather's birth certificate it states that his father
    was a laborer and his mother a domestic.
My ancestors were slaves.
In servitude to others.
They were caregivers, sailors, cooks, musicians, teachers and
    healers.
They were born into a life of service that was expected and
    necessary.
Serve and survive or die.

They all called my grandmother
"Mammy." She cared for, as she put it, "white people's
    children." Spoken more as a fact, but with a tinge of
    bitterness that she did not spend her days loving on her
    own six beautiful, brown children.

So what might be the upturning remnants of slavery that play
    out in a lifetime when you are a descendant of slaves?

Due to my mother's illness when I was eight years old, I
    became her child caregiver in service to my mother because
    she needed me until I eagerly left her house at 17 years
    of age.
Hurting, angry and with something important to prove.
Therapy would mean I was broken, crazy and in desperate
    need of the help of others.
That I was not.
Beautiful and young, I prided myself with being independent,
    self reliant and capable.
I continued living my life to find I landed in variations of
    service.
Did I uncover my true vocation? Did I find what I am
    gifted at?
Or did my ancestors groom me for a life of servitude?
Joining society's views and values that fit what a black woman
    can become.
Overlooking or unable to see beyonthe stereotypes of a
    cleaner, nanny, cook, caregiver, birth worker.
Basically fitting any construct that includes giving of oneself
    to meet other's needs is an acceptable role to fill in the eyes
    of dominant culture for a black woman and ensures safety
    and survival.

I sank into a comfortable life based on the concept that giving
    was a way of surviving.
Providing value and being needed equated playing out some
    dysfunctional pattern.
I felt undeserving and emotional when becoming the recipient
    of any unrequited goodness.

Somewhere inside knowing that there must be a truer way to be. I now acknowledge that emptying all the reserves is not a long term sustainable way to habituate and thrive without encountering stress, burnout and illness.

In honor of my ancestor's hard work towards freedom, I must continue to move in the progressive direction of getting free. Free of the remnants of slavery created by a system of white supremacy.

Fed by greed.
Still running its agenda through me.
Which means I'm examining standards I have accepted for myself within all my current relationships.
Asking difficult questions like:
How am I received when I am meeting my needs?
Am I welcome when I'm not giving?
Am I invited because my presence soothes?
Am I supported with no expectation?

Recently I saw an illuminated sign on the front of a city bus.
OUT OF SERVICE. Not that the bus had no purpose. It was simply taking no passengers at this time.
Giving clear information that being of service is a choice.
I asked myself.
What if I am out of service to others and being supported in service to myself? Or at least able to find a balance where one consciously feeds the other.

The gift of choosing to be in service to myself requires a precise set of circumstances.
Safety. Trust. Time. Connection.
Willingness to ask and receive.

The possibilities then cascade into expression and right action beginning with myself rippling out to others as a template for a new way of living.

An action of support may release my ancestors from their shackles.

An action of support may bring abundance and freedom to future generations of my lineage.

An action of support may allow me to live out my days without the invisible bondage of indebtedness to others.

An action of support may simply mean me living a creative life.

I will welcome meeting my ancestors when my time comes knowing that I did my part in our families generational evolution.

Right now I choose to honor me and be in service to myself.

I still don't really know what freedom means.

I still don't know where freedom will lead me.

But I do know I'm ready.

I dream of feeling freedom.

Feeling wholly, welcomed and received.

My marker for this experience of freedom is the still tangible memory of the embrace of my grandmother's unconditional love.

I know there in her arms I am accepted as I am.

Free to forever be me.

Reflection

How are you in a transactional relationship with yourself?

Who are you in service to?

EXPECTATIONS

Using conscious energy to work towards being free of self-
  made expectations.
A voice only I hear constantly whispers.
"Push beyond.
You don't need help.
You will do more."
A lurking voice full of oppressive expectations screams.
"You are an addict!
Being needed equates being indispensable."
I toss the table upside down.
Welcoming burnout.
All the game pieces now arranged.
What if passion is my work?
What if I choose to love myself first?
And my value is determined by time spent in communion with
  what pleasures me?
And when I give.
For no reason.
Maybe?
Then.
This mule is getting free.

Reflection

Where is your passion visible to the world?

How do you prioritize your joy?

CHAMPION

Meeting confusion.
Hatred filled with fears.
Step after step on uncharted maps you walk.
Don't disappear now.
Hatred hurts.
Walk the unknown way with stars as your compass.
Cultivate the plethora of melanin gifts within.
Timing for truth is important.
I need you here, now.
We need you here, now.

This is the long game.
Believing.
Wounded Warrior, you are not wrong.
Fallen champion unhinge this heavy armor.
Lay down weapons.
Fighting fear against fear is a futile combat strategy.
Healing weaponry will lead the way.

Champion with a stand-alone spirit.
Let your chosen army lift one another up in joy.

Wielding your medicine moment by moment.
Slough off dead, worn-out skin.
It no longer serves.
That's not a champion's garment to wear.
Polish the golden armor of your cultured soul.
Expand a crucible of fire so large all can see you.

Ancestors left trails of jewels to follow.
Rendezvous in that crack of light.
Lean in.
Feel it's weight.
Cry tears of vulnerability until your whole self rises like cream
    moving slowly to the top overflows.
Sink into ancestral memory.
You are enough as you are.
You are enough.

Always a champion smiling from a place of inner wealth.
Casting generous seeds of inspiration across many lands.
Survivor.
Sole protector of those hidden wounds.
Bearer of years of burdens.
Maybe no one hears you now.
May your silent words move mountains.
May your soul fly free.
Rest and be free.
Truly free.

Reflection

What are melanin gifts?

How are you protecting and defending?

WE ARE HUMANS

The privilege of my skin color is evident on rare occasions.
I've grown comfortable with apparent discomfort in proximity
    to whiteness.
Within spaces and places of mostly brown people I fit,
    disappear, become anonymous.
Can be referred to as *a queen* in the royal sense.
Become someone's mother, sister, adopted family for a week.
Once at a concert I stalked past backstage security to meet one
    of my favorite African bands.
No one blinked an eye. Racial likeness to the appearance of the
    band was my ticket to ride that day.
Often I am the ONLY brown one in the room. Partly
    choice or is it an uncanny ability to play out my ancestral
    patterning (choosing to pioneer white places and spaces) so
    well I have come to believe in the statement: "I belong."
Someone asks.
"WHAT ARE YOU ANYWAY?" I like to convince myself
    curiosity and genuine interest fuel this question.
I've heard it my whole life.
The violating penetration referring to my ancestry, cafe au
    lait skin color, look, gender, British accent and more .....
    Expectation for me to comply with an answer is REAL.
Maybe knowing which box I fit into helps judgement EASE
    into understanding and acceptance?
I'm not black enough or white enough. I have "good" hair and
    lighter skin.

Am I a threat or a reminder of the wounds of the past?
I don't know.
I'm simply **VELDA** working on being me.
Finding complex camaraderie in my brown-ness.
Simultaneously feeling anger and pride in the human pull to be an ally for ones who are oppressed and excluded **IF** I am accepted.
The confusion of where I fit or belong continues to work razor-like emotional edges.
My black grandparents used to say, "All **GOOD** people are welcome at our table."
They never told me what "good" meant to them. I never thought to ask.
I belong to **ME** within this — my current body of self.
Continually embracing diversity and connecting multiple different similarities in concrete ways.
I still believe in love, joy and freedom for all.
We are human. Aren't we?

Reflection

How are you reminded of the wounds of the past?
What makes you feel belonging?

FEELING BROWN

I'm feeling so *brown*.
"Brown like sweet exotic spiced sugar or like a dirty, limp used
    rag?" asks my Melanin Muse.
I ponder the light with .....
Brown like thickened cacao coating my throat. The brown part
    of me born of the original humans.
From an abundant continent able to satisfy scarcity's ravenous
    appetite.
Kings dressed in robes of rich, bright cloth that smile, dance
    and are fiercely loving.
Queens full of wild laughter and song. Walking with heads
    held high, as if floating on air with their pride of princes
    and princesses trailing behind them. Ready to bite with eyes
    on fire in an instant.
Or/And I acknowledge the dark with ....
The dirty brown that feels mucky and inadequate. With
    unnamed shame bubbling to the surface of the skin. Brown
    on the outside but trying to be another color inside to fit
    the outside.
Blushing and flushing with confused discomfort. Shrinking
    and expanding into bodies that don't fit or don't exist yet.
Looking around the room for some likeness.
A nod of recognition.
Nothing.
No one is brown like me.
Not here. Not now. Not today.

Sensitivity plus consciousness is a load to carry within a life
    trying to work through an equation that may never be neat
    and solved.
Melanin Muse interrupts. "Hold up there. The way I see it
    you can begin with relishing in all sides of your *feeling brown,*
    for that is loving self.
You, brown, human, Velda."
I'm just wondering.
Are you feeling *black, brown or white*?

Reflection

What helps you empathize with other racial identities?

URGENCY

It took about 5 weeks of being away from home to hear my
inner rhythms. Waking later.
Or just lying in bed longer. Staying in pjs till noon. Eating
when hungry.
Sleeping deeply and waking rested with a smile on my face.
There is no need to rush.
The world turns with or without me.
Time and urgency can rest awhile.
What does not get done today can always happen tomorrow.
Breathe in where you are. Breathe out any residue of
impatience, urgency and panic.
Nature knows her own timing.
A time for dormancy and darkness.
A time for the expansion of life.
A time for harvest and fruit.
A time for compost and decay.
A time for deep healing.
That is now.
The sense of urgency to do more or be more is a lie.
Urgency is oppressive.
Urgency opposes presence.
Urgency kills.
Urgency brings up feelings of confusion in the speed of light.
Confusion because I am outside of my skin looking for the
entry again.
Opposing urgency is authenticity.

Blood rushing.
Stress, anxiety and worry based on a feeling of lack.
Lack of time to get my perception of *everything* done in a day.
Lack of connection to what matters most.
In dog-like fashion I chase my tail to catch up with myself.
Going nowhere.
To be still, center, relax and connect to those who are right
    in front of me — disrupted by streaming random thoughts
    and inner agitation.
So I move from there to here and back again.
Busying myself.
Nervous system on fire.
Feeling that I'm missing something or meant to be somewhere
    else doing so much more.
Like putting myself out there. Being famous. Making money.
Addicted to processing my inner world. Hashing out fine
    details with all who question or care to listen.
But. I already am more and a single moment is more than
    enough time to be a difference.
If taking time is my new style.
Nothing is ever urgent.
Until it is.
So now.
I.
Be.

Reflection

How do you find yourself working with urgency
or dominant culture's confining ideals?

BLACK

No need to corral, police, parent or fix.
I am black,
When I say black I am talking African descent with brown skin.
The only lineage I know is black.
Unfamiliar with my white bloodline.
I reject connection to my white ancestry.
Just as it divested me.
Who is responsible is also accountable. Right?
Pumped up as a unique hybrid mongrel.
That's an inner defense tactic created to bolster myself in a
    culture that is fond of categorizing and judging based on
    skin color.
Defining me as less.
Because I am black?
Sometimes I call myself brown. That is the true color of
    my skin.
Or is brown a dilution?
Living in a country that exhibits racist values.
Within a majority brown-skinned fucking world.
I believe that character and heapings of self-love matter.
Self-identifying in variations of blackness.
Scared of being seen as only black.
I am a human chameleon continually code-shifting to fit the
    many adapting colors of an environment.

QUEENDOM

Welcome to my Queendom.

The area where my energy permeates everything.

This place is all things soft and strong. Light and dark. Deep and wide.

The bass winding up my waist in a celebratory dance of this sacred magic of being alive.

My passion is potent.

Wildness easily accessible through the rhythm of a drum.

My voice will sound a welcome song that makes you blush a little to receive so much intimate attention.

No holding back.

I hold your hands in mine.

A crackle of lightning belly-laughter vibrates — taking up all the space and tears of wet joy — trickling down our cheeks.

We are together.

Love will not be contained or repressed in my Queendom.

I govern in a way that clearly pleasures me.

Ample time, sensitivity and warmth overflowing.

I welcome you into this palace with an embrace that holds the universe.

The rules are fluid.

The high standards of kindness and respect revered.

Safety permeates the atmosphere.

Eye contact slipping into comfortable silence.

There is abundance to share.

A blanket, an open ear, cozy hat, words of encouragement, warm tea, clear guidance and spicy family curry.

Rest your laurels here my friend.

Confidence oozes from the cushions on the couch, the carpet holds you to the earth and the painted walls are ready to receive you.

The cake baking in the oven contains brandy-soaked fruit, ritually prayed over for a whole year.

Sweetness fills the lungs of this small palace I call home.

When I smile at you, warm sunshine lights up the air and kisses your gentle face.

Just like my grandma smiled at me.

You will always be treasured just as you are.

In my Queendom.

Reflection

How do you live in your Queendom or Kingdom?

BLACK WOMANHOOD

A black woman stepping into internalized aspects of racism.

Which for good reason were too heinous to bear before now.

The times right now have opened the vault.

I can smell my own fears.

Waiting for the barricaded dam to burst open with years of
    tears that haven't come yet.

My body always tells the truth.

There is a wedge embedded in my heart. Self-loathing is in
    each pore of my skin.

Self-love feels like a superfluous construct of the mind made
    for someone who doesn't look like me.

I like who I am. My skin, my name.

That is what smiles on the surface of the water.

Below the surface, the truth is I loathe what the system says it
    means to be a black woman in this body, in this world.

I wonder what self love feels like?

Reflection

How are you nurturing blackness?
What helps access self love?

UNDER ELEMENTS

Let **POWER** charge through you.
Step bravely into true autonomous strength feeding your soul
   from the core of the earth.
Source power is infinitely available.

Let **FLUIDITY** move you.
Tears creating space for life to burst forth.
Be like seagrass in warm salt water.
Gentle, tender but strong enough to move freely with
   every current.
Float your resonant magic throughout time.

Let **WARMTH** penetrate as the sun's outer rays kiss melanin
   in skin.
While inner fire is kindling.
Ignited by bold imagination to spark change.
Hold vigil in your spacious womb of creation.
Dream yourself a new reality.
Go on.
Rename yourself.

Let **LIGHT** fill and surround you arriving at a place where the
   weight of history becomes air in your bones.
Laugh, smile, giggle, find levity in each step of the journey.
Generosity flowing in action.

BIRTH RITES

What is already mine?
Coming here with distant, yet familiar recollections, then
    forgetting everything.
Finding.
Drum beat, feathers, sweet animal breath on skin.
Earth smells, warm sand sifting through hands and mud
    between toes.
Satisfaction with being self.
Sacred full vessel.
Allowing.
A stillness and quiet that comes through the ears and
    permeates one's being.
Hear the heart's steady rhythm beating in the open spaces.
Breath slow, deep, filling completely again and again.
Emptying.
Echoing sound so primal it springs salty tears.
Joy bubbling over and over again.
Onto soft cheeks.
Delicious truth moving within a physical body.
Claiming.
No pretending.
Courage to step into what is right.
Recalling an essential source.
Explore the landscape of inner terrain.
Look long enough into eyes and see self reflected.
Potential with infinity.
The gifts of one's birth rites.

PROLOGUE

Writing words offers me a space to be unfiltered. My self. I dip
into streams of ancestral blood on this planet earth. My work
in the world is spiritual, primal and healing. I have helpers.
It is a collaborative essence that graces these pages informed
by the elements of fluidity and place with spirit. I live with
the knowledge of what is presented on the outside. Face, skin,
body has little to do with the content found within a person's
soul. I am an observant seeker of the unseen and inaudible
gifts in all my earthly encounters.

I live with the knowledge that what is presented is only part of
the obvious truth.

BIOGRAPHY IN ARCHETYPES

Born. The responsible indebted **INNOCENT** child.
Confused about love becoming.
The willing **CAREGIVER.**
Giving power over to it and becoming.
The used one. Named Velderella.
There was no.
HERO. Protector of the underdog. This was how I perceived
   myself.
Then.
The **HEALER** constantly flows with nurturing loving
   kindness.
Willing to support and guide all beings.
I became **EVERYMAN.**
The **LOVER** survived and shared all things humanly beautiful
   in as many ways possible.
So the **CREATOR** came into the light and emerged trying to
   pass me gifts in the form of potent weapons to cut through
   the layers of illusion.
Urgency invoked the patient **SAGE** who began to understand
   that living the lesson is the long game and timing means
   everything.
The **OUTLAW** continued to feel alone never fitting in or
   belonging even in her own skin.
The **RULER** kept pushing new standards until they became
   palatable to the difference maker.
The **MAGICIAN** emerged as an energy shaper sounding the
   energy of matter into being.
The **JESTER** is present now bringing levity and humor to the
   horrid, mundane and sacred.

ACKNOWLEDGEMENTS

I am an incredibly blessed person to have been born at a time where it is possible for me to uncover more of who I truly am and manifest it as I feel it coming through me. I am birthing myself again and again, then putting parts to rest, peeling the fine layers away, letting go again and again. I am finding more stillness, strength and clarity as I continue to walk my soul's path and purpose. I am blessed with courage and the consciousness to face myself. If I am fortunate, I am left with something to share: be it art, sound, support, presence, performance or simply the primal essence of my own human nature. I am honored to share what is here, right now, with you in this moment.

I thank my muse for consistently tapping me on the shoulder to remind me that words are my love.

I acknowledge my rigorous inner critic because from dwelling in those depths I managed to emerge with more to say. I bow down and kiss the giving lands upon which I have been fortunate enough to walk and live. Much gratitude for the exhale of generations of ancestors who forged this path for me to now tread. And I must acknowledge the inbreath of brave new souls arriving on this earthly plane. I shower blessings to a multitude of individuals for their encouragement. Engaging me with lively conversation and listening ears as I talked myself in spirals towards healing inspiration. This I will never forget. Thank you to my beautiful children for showing me there is strength in vulnerability. My husband for his clarity and grounded strength.

And my larger family. For seeing who I am, allowing me to be and holding me always in love.

Finally, thanks to all those who have made this book possible, with apologies for any omissions.

Holly Madrone, Oceana Sawyer, Jessica Morrell, Martha Swain, Erinn Kauer, Rae Kala, Lisa Flanders, Karolina Anderson, Zhaleh Almaee, Lisbeth White, Neave Karger, Kay Jensen, Randelle Hamm, Lauren Green, Liz Quayle, Hanna Onnemyr Cole, Dena Renea Evans, Ahmad Baabahar, Strait Up Magazine, Joanne Hafner, Alexandra Heiser, JCARF, Nala Walla, TKB, Nicole Larson, Renee Collier, Susanna Reynolds, Kavi Baabahar, Suzy Carroll, Clayton William, Bob Triggs, Kreea Baabahar, Giovanna Tomasi, Torii Rom, Barbara Morgan, Radha Newsome, Shirley Scheier, Ashnie Butler, Joanne Murayama, Jen Goff, Dawn Reardon, Brenda Bole, Camelia Jade, Sam, Madeline Leach, Sarah Jane, Monica Aebi, Jennimae Hillyard, Jude Rubin, Janet Lia, Jill Alban, Arendt Speser, Rose Burt, Lindsay Scalf, Molly Stebbins, Jane Rioseco, Nathan Land, Catherine Herrick, Lisa Leporati, Damiana Paternoster, Annalisa Barrelli, Crystie Kisler, Aba Kiser, Lexi Koch, Local Dairy Council, Tara Baabahar, Afrose Fatima Ahmed, Shirley Smith, Rikki Ducornet, Anthony Prud'homme, Jeanette Stengel, Aletia Anna Alvarez, Abby Jorgensen, Sarah Whitney, Sidonie Maroon, Diane Ginther

Special thanks to those who support me on Patreon.

A Brief Friendship was originally printed in *Strait Up Magazine*, Issue 4, 2020

VELDA THOMAS. Born and educated in England, UK with biracial family ancestry sourced from Africa, the Caribbean and the Americas. Healing modalities have always been of interest. Love of plants, herbal remedies, somatic and ritual experiences weave passion with grounded human experience for creativity and freedom of expression. Velda has worked as a kindergarten teacher, adult educator, birth doula, massage therapist, sound practitioner and writer. Velda is a horsewoman, nature lover, mover of the body and world traveler. Currently living in Port Townsend on the Olympic Peninsula, USA.

This book was published in August 2021
by Stardust Press.
The text was set in Mrs Eaves,
designed by Rose Burt,
printed and bound by Gorham Printing
in Centralia, WA.

First Stardust Edition of 1000 copies,
each numbered and signed by the author.
All rights reserved.

375/1000

Stay Connected
veldathomas@hotmail.
com
veldathomas.com

STARDUST PRESS